THE CRADLE OF

AMERICAN

AVIATION

THE NATIONAL AVIATION FIELD
COLLEGE PARK, MD.

BY KEN BEATTY

HBP

952 FREDERICK ST., P.O. BOX 190, HAGERSTOWN, MD. 21740

First Edition
Copyright © 1976 Ken Beatty
No portion of this book may be reproduced without written permission of the author
Library of Congress No. 76-26831
Printed in U.S.A. 1976
Hagerstown Bookbinding and Printing Co.
Hagerstown, Maryland 21740

Dedication

IN MEMORY OF ALL THOSE MEN AND WOMEN WHO DEDICATED THEIR LIVES AND ENERGY THAT MAN MIGHT FLY

Here on this hallowed field as I stand and watch the sun rise and the gentle breeze push back the morning haze, there is a feeling that I am not alone. It is as if the spirits of those early aviators and mechanics come each day with the rising sun to continue their efforts to lift men to the heavens. As the first rays of the sun reflect off the hangar roof covered with dew, it is as though the Lord has placed a diamond crown upon it as a reward for her many accomplishments. No other place in this country has so richly deserved the title of THE CRADLE OF AMERICAN AVIATION. Maybe someday, men will erect a fitting monument to her many achievements.

Until that time it is with great pleasure that I dedicate this book to all those men and women who gave their lives and energies that man might fly.

Ken Beatty

Preface

At the insistence of my many good friends, I have taken pen in hand in order to compile many of the historic facts that I uncovered while serving as Director of the National Aerospace Educational Memorial Center, College Park, Maryland. In my opinion there is no other site in these United States, which more richly deserves the title THE CRADLE OF AMERICAN AVIATION than the College Park Airport. It is not only our nation's first federally recognized airport but also the oldest continually operating airport in the world.

Many books have been written about the history of aviation and I'm sure many more will follow. However, this book is not written for the aviation buff or the historian, although I'm sure it will become a must on their reading lists; rather, this book is written to inform the average person of the many firsts that took place at the National Aviation Field at College Park. Many persons who live in College Park and the surrounding area have said they had no idea of the important events that occurred there, and many, although they knew there was an airport, had never been there. To these persons, and others like them across our broad land, I hope this book will be informative.

Most history books have pages of reading and, occasionally, a photograph or two to illustrate a point. However, in setting out to do this book I felt it more important to reverse the tradition and leave a more lasting visual image in the mind of the reader. I must apologize for the quality of some of the photographs for they are very old and in some cases even spotted or damaged. A close study of the details of the people and the backgrounds will reveal a story all of its own.

It is also my intention to hopefully correct some eroneous information which has been circulated in the past even to the extent of possibly destroying monumental markers erected by would-be do-gooders. It should be made perfectly clear at this point that, although many years of research and personal interviews have gone into the preparation of this book, some items were taken from heresay or the recollection of persons who were there. Many photographs were given to me by persons who claimed they had been taken at College Park and to the best of my limited ability they seemed authentic. Anyone having a contrary or new or additional information are invited to contact the museum curator at the airport, and perhaps the future editions can be updated.

The collection of photographs which you are about to view will enable you to relive those glorious days of yesteryear when man was first learning to fly. Those brave and daring young men risked everything on a flimsy contraption of spruce, canvas, and wire and without aid of seatbelts, compasses, parachutes, or the modern luxuries that we enjoy today, to blaze a trail as the pioneers of American aviation. If you will be bear with my humble attempts as a writer, I shall lead you down the path of history to visual and verbal images of that glorious past.

ACKNOWLEDGMENTS

It is with grateful appreciation that I take this opportunity to personally thank and recognize all those many persons who helped to make this book possible. Without their assistance, information, and understanding these historic facts may have gone unrecorded. Not wishing to omit anyone for any reason, but limited to time and space, my thanks.

Special Thanks To:

Miss Chapman, Robert Higdon . . . Det 5, HQ Aerospace Audio-Visual Service, U.S.A.F.

Virginia G. Finci, Chief . . . Research Service Unit, 1361st P.S. AAUS.

Dr. Paul Garber, Lou Casey . . . Smithsonian Air and Space Museum

Fred Knauer, Ken Lewis . . . National Aerospace Educational Memorial Center

Dr. Walter Zarahavitz . . . National Aerospace Education Council

Maj. Gen. Dale Smith, Col. David Enyard . . . Air Force Historical Society

Research Staff . . . The National Archives & Record Service

Bill Aleshire, Chairman . . . College Park, Adelphi and Prince Georges County Jaycees

Mr. Schiek & Staff . . . Maryland-National Capital Park and Planning Commission

Historical Records Division . . . U.S. Post Office Department

William W. Gullett . . . former mayor of College Park, and Prince Georges County Executive

George and Jeff Brinkerhoff . . . College Park Airport, College Park, Maryland

Ron Freeman . . . Executive Aviation

Henry A. Berliner, Theodore Richardson, Steuart Reiss, Majorie Huxley Silver

Mr. & Mrs. Robert H. Sauter and Son

Members of the National Aerospace Cadets

Members of the Mud Flat Falcons

Lt. Claude Morse, Douglas J. Wagner, James C. Powell, Jr. . . . Photographers

Jim Stahl, Vonda Henninger, Penny Smith, Martha Jane Reid, Audrey Beatty . . . My Staff

Table of Contents

Chapter I
Events Leading To College Park

The Wright Brothers did not by chance happen to stumble on the airplane. For years they read and studied all of the books they could find by inventors like Lilenthal and Langley and they wrote letters requesting specific information on aeronautical problems. They built scale models and even perfected their own wind tunnel. Their selection of Kitty Hawk, North Carolina as the testing sight for their gliders and later powered aircraft was a direct result of research for a constant wind velocity to keep their craft afloat.

A-Orville Wright USAF Photo

B-Wilbur Wright USAF Photo

Any schoolchild can tell you that College Park was NOT the sight where the Wright Brothers first flew their planes, but Kitty Hawk was also not an airport and didn't even have a paved landing strip until the 1960's. Therefore it certainly cannot claim the title of Our Nation's first and the World's oldest operating landfield.

After their successful flight at Kitty Hawk the Wright Brothers returned to Dayton Ohio where they got permission from a banker, Torrence Huffman, to use his pasture for their flying experiments. In 1904 and 1905, they tested and improved their plane during the early morning hours when they could not be observed by sightseers. The field lay at the intersection of the main road between Dayton and Springfield and the road running to Yellowsprings, Ohio. An electric line ran along one side of the field between Dayton and Springfield.

By May 23, 1905, they were assembling a NEW machine in a newly constructed building on the field which became their Dayton factory. No flights were made from this field from 1906 until November 1909 (after College Park) when the Wright Company of the United States opened its flying school near Montgomery, Alabama and Huffman field. In 1917 the old Wright Field was called McCook Field until 1927. Likewise in 1917 another field was started, called Patterson Field. These two fields were merged to form the present-day Wright-Patterson A.F.B. which does not have a continuous record of service from its beginning in 1904. In 1939 the old factory hangar was torn down, and the area is not being used today as an airport. The Wright's also flew from polo grounds, parks, and any other field where they could or had to land even in Europe, but to my knowledge none of these are operating air fields today as is College Park.

C-Now standing side by side in Greenfield Village at the Edison Institute at Dearborn, Michigan are the restored Dayton, Ohio home and shop of the Wright Brothers where they carried on their research into aeronautical problems and perfected the first heavier-than-air flying machine. USAF Photo

A
From 1901-1903 the Wright Brothers conducted glider test flights from the sand dunes at Kitty Hawk, North Carolina. It was here that they developed their wing warping method for turning their craft. This photo is their 1902 version. USAF Photo.

B
The first flight by man with a motor-driven heavier-than-air machine was at Kitty Hawk, North Carolina on December 17, 1903. Since it had no wheels it was launched from a greased rail (note bucket in lower right corner). USAF Photo

C
The Wright Brothers Memorial . . . Located at Kill Devil Hill, Kitty Hawk, North Carolina. General contours of the hill are virtually the same as in the 1902 glider flights and the first powered flight in 1903. Prevailing breezes came off the ocean in upper right corner of photo. USAF Photo

A-As part of the original contract with the government for an aeroplane, it had to be transportable by wagon. USAF Photo

B-The Wright plane in hangar at Ft. Myer, Va., June 28, 1909. Hangar was built especially for these tests on the parade grounds. USAF Photo

C-Assembling the plane for flight. Note detachable steel wheels used to roll plane to launch rail. USAF Photo

D-Attaching ropes on catapult rail. Note sightseers and autos in background. USAF Photo

E-Engine warm-up and check out of control surfaces. USAF Photo

F-Ready for takeoff, Lt. Lahm with Orville Wright at controls July 27, 1909. Note officer with stop watch checking time. USAF Photo

A
September 12, 1908, Orville Wright stays aloft for one hour and fourteen minutes as part of army requirements for flights lasting over one hour. Tents were erected for quarters and office. Mounted troops were required to keep crowds back. USAF Photo

B
September 17, 1908, Lt. Thomas E. Selfridge and Orville Wright crash when propeller breaks, sheering guide wire and causing tail to droop. Orville had a broken thigh and Selfridge died three hours later; this was our nation's first aviation fatality in a military aircraft.

C
The old Wright Hangar, Dayton, Ohio. Photo taken October 17, 1939 just before hangar was torn down. It had been many years since it had been used. USAF Photo

Chapter II
The Army Flying School

If we were to really affix a date for the beginning of aviation at College Park Airport, we would have to return to a period in time before the military selected it for their use. For many years the pleasant valley had watched the early efforts of man learning to fly. From a nearby countryside near Bladensburg, Thaddeus S. Lowe first tethered his balloon the Entreped to inform Union forces of the advancing Confederate attack on the Nation's Capital in 1862. His cabled messages went directly to President Abraham Lincoln in the White House.

1907, on the same field where the airport now stands, it was reported that Alexander Graham Bell stopped his horse and carriage to observe Fred Fox being towed behind a horse on a huge 20′ x 30′ man-carrying kite about 100 feet in the air. Some persons believe this is where Bell conceived the ideas for his kite experiments. Old-timers in the area recall the incident but were unable to affix a date to it.

A-Army Contract for first plane, National Archives Photo

The three parts of the army contract called for the plane to be portable on the ground by wagon and to carry a passenger and travel at 40 miles per hour while staying aloft for over one hour; the third part was the training of two military officers to be pilots. The first two were accomplished at Ft. Myer, Va. However, the Post Commander became very upset with all the crowds and at having to use so many men for guard duty to keep spectators off the field, to say nothing of the fact that the planes were frightening the calvary horses during training. So he instructed the men to take that **!! machine off his post.

Lt. Lahm was a signal corps balloonist and since his unit was now assigned to Capt. Chandler's Aeronautical Unit, he was instructed to go aloft and find a new sight. Drifting in free ascent towards Baltimore he observed the Rex Smith Hangar and Aeroplane. Descending, he borrowed a horse and rode to the site where the airport is located today.

B-Lt. Frank P. Lahm, USAF Photo

C-Lt. Frederic Humphreys, USAF Photo

D-Lt. Benjamin D. Foulois, USAF Photo

A-Lt. Lahm and his balloon and crew at Fort myer, Va. National Archives Photo

B-Land Lease Agreement for College Park Airport. Page one of eleven page contract. National Archives Photo

October 1903, not too many miles to the west of the airport along the banks of the beautiful Potomac River, James Pierpoint Langley was conducting his experiments with his famous catapulting aircraft that met with an unfortunate mechanical mishap.

C
War Dept. Order dated July 3, 1909 established U.S. Signal Corps Aviation School at College Park, Maryland. The school was located near the town of College Park, about 7 miles from Washington, D.C. The site chosen by the military was southeast of the town. The 160-acre field was leased on August 25, 1909. The area was bordered on the west by the B and O Railroad, (where our Nation's first railroad & telegraph connecting two cities was located), on the north and east by the Paint Branch & the eastern branch of the Potomac River, and on the south by Calvert Road. The longest runway was 2,376 feet in an east- to west direction. The Quartermaster Department of the Army paid $325. per month for the land. First, two hangars were constructed from a drawing by Mr. Wright on the back of an envelope given to an army engineer. In 1910, with the purchase of the Curtiss Plane SC #2, two more hangars were added. Two were for the planes and 2 were for the enlisted officers who lived in D.C. All four hangars were 45 feet square. On August 19, 1911, orders were given to construct two larger hangars, 51 feet square (see attached drawing). This was our nation's first military airfield and the first area recognized by the government as an airport.

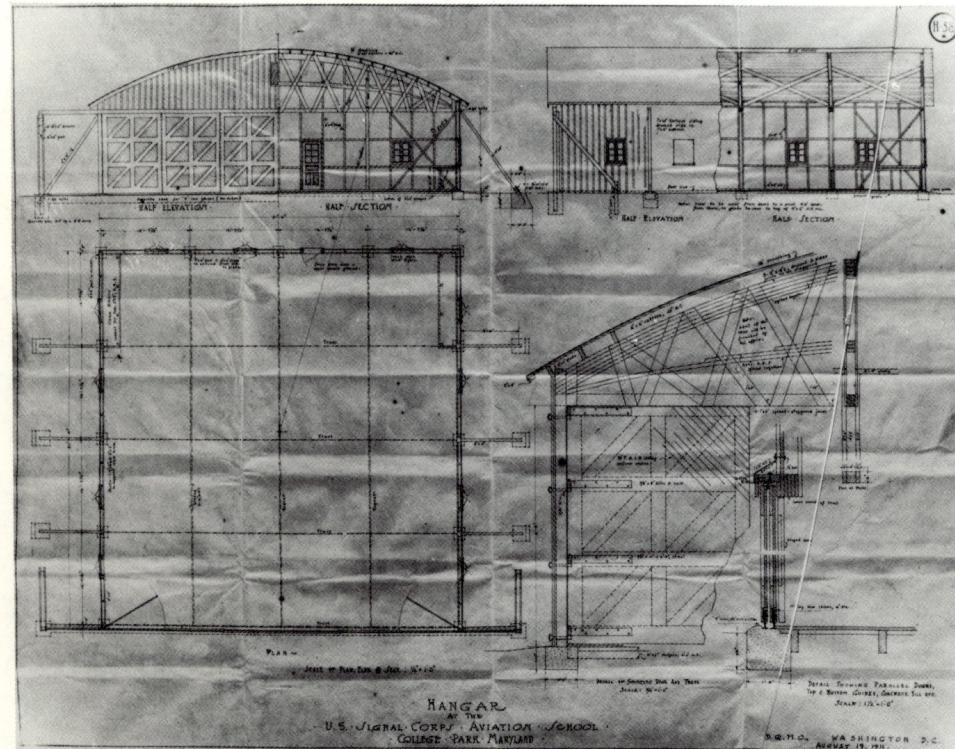

On the left you see Lts. Lahm and Humphreys with Wilbur Wright as they make their first survey of the new field. It was decided at this time that Rex Smith's (2) hangars would have to be moved closer to Calvert Road in order to make more room for the army's needs. August 2, 1909, the U.S. Army accepts the world's first military plane. Contract agreements were completed at College Park with the training of two military officers as flight instructors. USAF Photo

On the right is Lt. Benjamin D. Foulois who was to have been one of the officers to receive flight training, however, he was sent to Nancy, France to observe aviation achievements at the International Congress of Aeronautics September 8 thru October 17, 1909. He returned to College Park after Lts. Lahm & Humphreys had received their training and flew as a passenger a few more times before the plane was damaged and was returned to the factory for repairs. NAEMC Photo

C

The Rex Smith Hangar and Flying School at College Park which had to be moved to make room for the Army's Hangars. Two signs are visible on the roof of the hangar "Christmas Aeroplane Company" and "Rex Smith Aeroplane Company." There is a flag pole on the front edge of the first ventilator which was used to tell the pilots the direction of the wind. The hangar appears in good condition. NAEMC Photo

D

In 1909 only two hangars were constructed but by 1910 two other hangars had to be constructed to house troops and the two planes the army had. By 1911 the army had four planes and a water tower. Officers lived in D.C. and commuted by train but the enlisted men were housed on the field. NAEMC Photo

A

Things were really growing at College Park. The Smith complex has grown to four buildings to match the four the military have. Calvert Road is unpaved in the foreground. NAEMC Photo

B

The muddy and bumpy road paralleling the railroad tracks leads to the army flying school. The skies overhead are getting crowded with planes. NAEMC Photo

C

In this view we see six army hangars with a plane in each. Squad tents are still part of the army life. The quartermaster corps has even added an automobile. USAF Photo

A

Crowds are still a problem as people journey from miles away to watch this new phenomenon of flight. Notice the unique engineering on the split hangar doors of the Rex Smith Hangar. NAEMC Photo

B

The Wright "B" Airplane at College Park in 1911. The Curtiss Pusher, which was the army's number two plane, can be seen in the background. USAF Photo

C

Lts. Roy C. Kirtland and H. H. Arnold buzz the airfield in the 1911 Wright plane. USAF Photo

A-Wreck of the Wright Pursuit Airplane at College Park in 1912. Any landing you can walk away from is a good landing but not always so good for the plane or mechanics who had to repair them. USAF Photo

B-Left to right: Lt. Henry H. Arnold, Arthur L. Welsh (civilian), Lt. Leyton Hazelhurst at College Park June 1912, Wright Airplane. USAF Photo

C-A. L. Welsh & Hazelhurst — wreck of Wright Type C at College Park in 1912. USAF Photo

D-Lts. "Hap" Arnold and Thomas DeWitt Milling receive their military aviators licenses at College Park in 1912. USAF Photo

E-Capt. Charles DeForrest Chandler in the Wright type airplane at College Park in June 1911. USAF Photo

F-Left to right: Arthur L. Welsh and Lt. Layton Hazelhurst at College Park in 1912. USAF Photo

A
Lt. Hap Arnold in Wright Type
C at College Park in 1911. Note
sandbags are believed to be part
of early bomb-dropping experiments at the field. USAF Photo

B
The Wright plane races the
train at College Park in 1909.
T. Richardson Photo

C
College Park, 1911 — Lt. Frank
M. Kennedy in the Curtiss
Trainer plane with tricycle
landing gear and ailerons.
USAF Photo

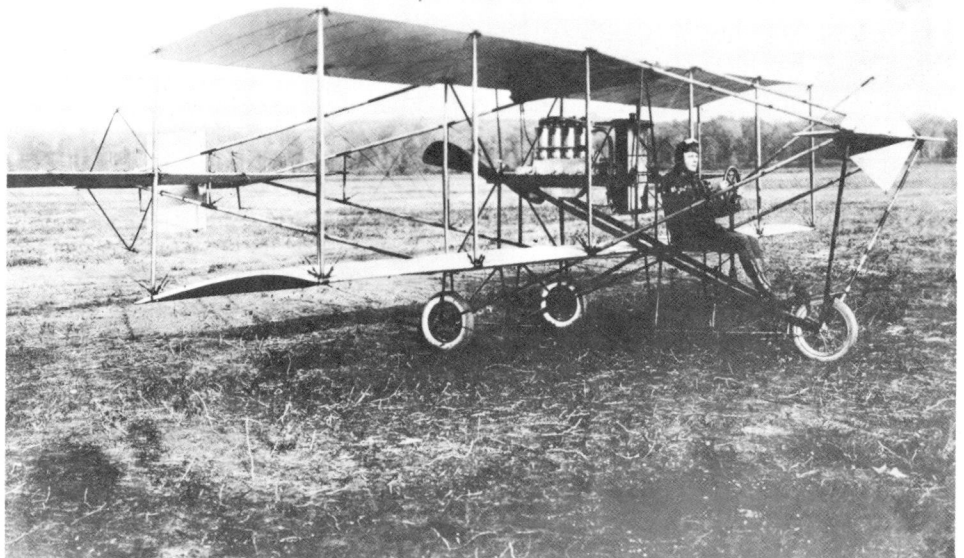

A
Ground crew pushes the Wright "C" out on the field early in the morning for flight training to avoid the crowds. USAF Photo

B
Preparing the plane for flight, Wilbur Wright works on engine. T. Richardson Photo

C
October 25, 1911, Lts. Arnold and Milling test of James Means visual signal device attached under wing which was not satisfactory. USAF Photo

A
This is how the 1909 Wright Scout appeared as it was being set up for the first time on the College Park Field. USAF Photo

B
Lt. Henry H. Arnold (right, in front seat) with 2 airplane mechanics from College Park about 1911. The car, a standard quartermaster issue for that period, is used to pull wagon hauling plane. USAF Photo

C
Aeronautical Board of the Signal Corps. Left to right: Lt. Frank P. Lahm, George C. Sweet (USN), Charles McK. Saltzman, Maj. George O. Squires, Capt. Charles DeForest Chandler, Benjamin D. Foulois, and Lt. Frederic E. Hummphreys. USAF Photo

A-Left to right: Harry Graham, Henry H. Arnold, Charles Def Chandler, Lincoln Beachey and Robert Moore with the Rex Smith airplane. USAF Photo

B-Capt. Beck, Lt. H. H. Arnold, Capt. C. D. Chandler, Lt. Thomas DeWitt Milling, and Lt. Roy Kirtland taken July 1911. USAF Photo

C-Capt. Hennessy, Lt. H. H. Arnold, Lt. Roy C. Kirtland, Capt. Frank M. Kennedy. Lt. McLeary, Lt. Harold Gerger, Lt. Thomas D. Milling and Lt. Lewis C. Rowkwell at College Park in 1911. USAF Photo

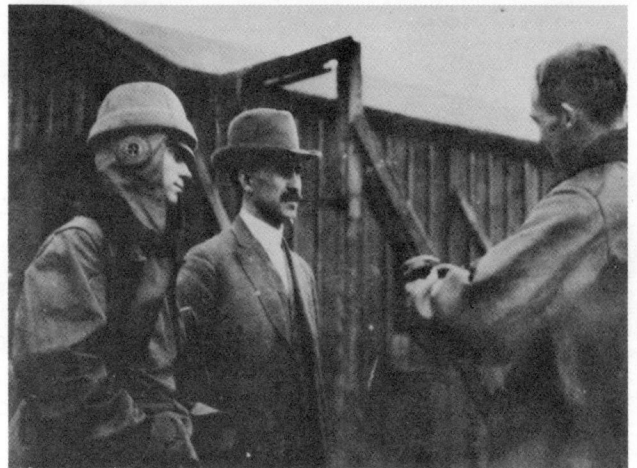

D-Orville Wright, Lt. T. D. Milling, and Lt. H. H. Arnold discuss engine modifications at College Park. USAF Photo

E-A composite of uniforms worn at College Park in May 1912. Left to right: Col. Winder, Lt. Hazelhurst, Lt. Milling, Capt. Beck, and Mr. Walsh. USAF Photo

F-Another 1915 group of pilots all wearing the leather aviators jackets. Left to right: Bowen, Carberry, Chapman, Foulois, Milling, and Rader. USAF Photo

Chapter III

History Making Events at College Park

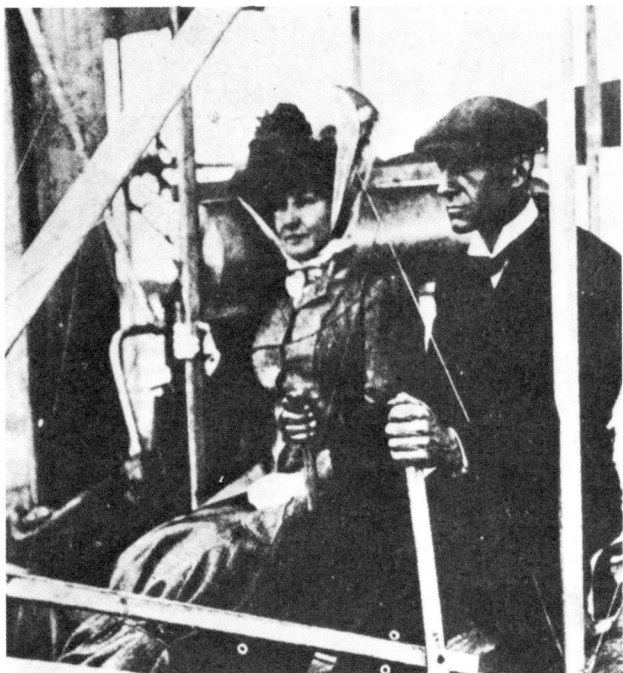

1ST woman in America to fly as a passenger was Mrs. Ralph H. Von Deman, wife of Capt. Von Deman of the 21st Infantry on October 27, 1909 at the College Park Airport. USAF Photo

1ST Naval Officer to fly in an airplane was Lt. George Cook Sweet who flew as a passenger with Lt. Lahm at College Park, November 3, 1909. USAF Photo

TWO CENTS.

NEAR DEATH IN AERO

Lieut. Arnold Benumbed by Cold at High Altitude.

MAKES NEW ARMY RECORD

Nearly Loses Control of Machine When 4,167 Feet in Air.

Strength of Will, However, Saves College Park Aviator From Being Dashed to Earth—Lieut. Kirtland, by Masterful Management of Aeroplane, Steps Into Ranks of Experts—Lieut. Milling Adds to Day's Total of Twelve Flights.

1ST person to fly a mile high (6,450 ft.), Lt. Henry "Hap" Arnold at College Park, 1912 in Wright "B" Airplane. USAF Photo

1ST machine gun fired from an airplane occurred at College Park on June 7, 1912 by Capt. Charles DeF. Chandler with Lt. Milling at the controls. USAF Photo.

1ST

dropping of live bombs from an airplane took place at College Park on October 10, 1911. Lt. Milling and Cpl. Riley E. Scott. USAF Photo

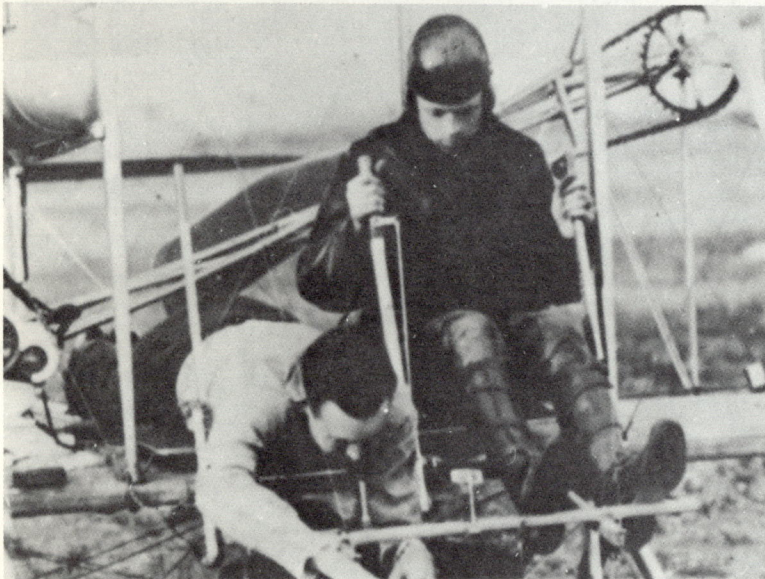

1ST

Bomb-dropping device developed and tested at College Park which won all prizes at Paris Air Show in 1912. USAF Photo

1ST

C

During the month of October 1911, wireless morse code messages were reportedly received by Dr. James Harris Rogers in his "Red Hill Receiving Station" in Hyattsville, several miles from the airport. Sources indicate that Lt. Foulois and Cpl. Scott were experimenting with wireless radio messages from their airplane above the field and were received by Dr. Rogers on several occasions. Dr. Rogers, an independent inventor and Nobel prize nominee, was experimenting with "Hydrophonics" in his lab behind what is now the County Service Building; his receiving station was located where the water tower now stands in Rogers Heights, the highest point of land between Baltimore and Washington, D.C. This communication took place about a month before the publicized 1st radio message from a plane at Fort Riley, Kansas. Gen. Pershing, it is believed, ordered the experiments classified until they could be demonstrated before the press at the huge war games on Nov. 2, 1912, in order to influence Congress to allot more money to the military.

1ST

aerospace medical team was established at College Park in October 1912 following the death of Cpl. Scott. The Adj. General of the Army recommended the assignment of a medical officer at the aviation field at College Park on June 14, 1911, however paperwork moved slowly in those days. Lt. Dr. John P. Kelley was recalled from Panama and assigned with a team of nurses to be present when flights were being made. Here you see their elaborate hospital tent and ambulance. NAEMC Photo

1ST

Air Mail Service. College Park became the Washington terminal for the United States first commercial air mail service August 12, 1918. Here you see aero-standard with air mail emblem on its side. It was also at College Park in 1919 that Douglas Fairbanks, Sr. affixed a stamp to his forehead and flew to Philadelphia to support a Liberty Bond Drive. Post Office Photo

1ST

controlled helicopter flight. From 1920 to 1924, Emile and Henry Berliner used the College Park airport to conduct their experiments in helicopter flight. Here you see his "G" version in a successful flight. This was nine years before Sikorsky's successful flights. NAEMC Photo

1ST aerial photo taken from an airplane was at College Park on September 19, 1911, 4:30 p.m., 600 ft. altitude. USAF Photo

B-Later air photo showing entire airport and hangars and gold fish ponds. NCAPPC Photo

C enlisted man killed in airplane accident was Cpl. Frank Scott at College Park on September 28, 1912. USAF Photo

1ST D-Cpl. Scott was buried in Arlington Cemetery. Here you can see the grave marker. NCAPPC Photo

Many other firsts occurred at College Park Airport: (no pictures)
- 1st Cross Country Formation Flight of three planes from College Park to Bethesda, Maryland and return nonstop.
- 1st Night Landing. Following the 1911 Army-Navy Football game, Capt. Charles DeForest Chandler had trouble getting his engine started and was delayed until 7:10 before he could take off for College Park. Facing strong headwinds, darkness engulfed the field before he could land. Alert and worried mechanics hastily poured gasoline along the sides of the runway so that he could see to land when they heard his plane approaching.
- 1st Aviation School where two military officers were taught to fly as well as Rex Smith's Flying School for civilians.
- 1st all-metal "Smooth Skin" aircraft built and test-flown at College Park, which was the prototype of the ercoupe.
- 1st landing and field lights developed for use during night landings on November 17, 1911.

- 1st experiments with blind landing equipment for fog and bad weather by the U.S. Bureau of Standards 1926-1933.

Chapter IV
The New Planes & Pilots

The first flights of the Wright Brothers did more than just create a news sensation; they kindled new visions and ideals in the minds and hearts of men. This 1910 drawing by G. H. Calvert, after whom Calvert Road is named, envisions the future use of air power to defend our nation. The Goddess of Flight is holding up a giant battle cruiser with three wings and a double horizontal stabilizer, powered by two tractor-type engines. Winging her way above the American Eagle, perched on the world globe, and surrounded by nature's champions of the sky, she is an outstanding example of man's visions of the future. NAEMC Photo

The following photographs in this chapter are but a few of the many that exist. If you observe closely you can see the rapid advancement in the technology of aviation that occurred at this historic field over a period of years: aircraft advances such as the change from pusher-type engines to tractor-type which pulled the planes through the skies; The change from water-cooled engines to air-cooled engines and from two-bladed propellers to three-bladed; from the Wright Brothers wing warping to ailerons and the moving of control surfaces from in front of the pilot to the rear of the plane. They added landing wheels, seat belts, and finally, a covered fuselage. Not all these improvements were invented at College Park but many improvements were tested here. As the planes became safer to fly, more and more persons took to the air, both military and civilians. The list of those notables who flew at College Park reads like a Who's Who of Flying: Wilbur Wright, Orville Wright, Rex Smith, Lts. Lahm, Humphries, and Foulois, Al Welch, Lincoln Beachy, Fred Orme, Tony Jannus, William Whitney Christmas, Paul Culver, Paul Peck, Henry Berliner, "Hap" Arnold and even Arthur Godfrey, to mention but a few. To some, flying at College Park was like singing at Carnegie Hall or the Met. Even actors of the silent movies like Douglas Fairbanks, Sr. flew from this mecca of aviation.

A-Test Pilot Kabitzki in the Wright Biplane, 1911. NAEMC Photo

B-Jay Safford cranking the Rex Smith Plane, 1911. NAEMC Photo

C-Capt. Benjamin D. Foulois in an Aerostandard plane. USAF Photo

D-Tony Januas with his reversed cap and goggles. Smithsonian Photo

A-Wright Type "C" airplane at College Park, 1912. USAF Photo

B-Tony Januas and the Rex Smith airplane, 1911. NAEMC Photo

C-The Curtiss Airplane, 1911 — Note other two planes in sky. NAEMC Photo

D-Lincoln Beachey at the wheel of the Curtiss pusher biplane with a 90 H.P. Curtiss OX engine. USAF Photo

E-The Columbia Monoplane near the Rex Smith Aeroplane Co. School. NAEMC Photo

F-A rear view of the Columbia Monoplane at College Park. NAEMC Photo

Rex Smith in the Rex Smith airplane 1911. Smithsonian Photo

Fred Fox also in the Rex Smith Plane. Smithsonian Photo

The Rex Smith airplane. Pilot Tony Jannus. Smithsonian Photo

The Wright "B" — with wheels which were the brainchild of O. G. Simmons, a military mechanic for Lt. Foulois at Ft. Sam Houston, Texas and improved at College Park. USAF Photo

Shortly after Lt. Foulois returned from France in 1909 he flew several times as a passenger with the Wright Brothers at College Park until the plane was badly damaged by one of the other military officers. The plane had to be sent to Dayton for repairs. Lts. Lahm & Humphries were assigned other duties and because of the severe weather at College Park during the winter months, Foulois was ordered to move his flight training to Ft. Sam Houston, Texas. After the plane was repaired, it was shipped by rail to the newly constructed hangar in Texas.

It was at this site that Lt. Foulois first took the controls of the plane and tried to apply all he had seen and learned at College Park. He would take off from the catapult rail and fly around learning to back and turn, but when he landed he stalled out and wrecked the plane. While repairs were being made with the aid of his mechanic O. G. Simmons, Lt. Foulois wrote to the Wright Brothers asking what he had done wrong. By the time the reply was received the plane was ready to go. Lt. Foulois repeated this process several times before he successfully learned to fly. So it could be said that he was the first aviator to learn to fly by correspondence. A "misleading" monument was later erected on that site which reads: "General Foulois, then a First Lieutenant of Signal Corps, made the first flight by an Army officer in a military plane at Fort Sam Houston on 2 March 1910." This statement is incorrect for Lts. Lahm and Humphries soloed as pilots at College Park. On October 26, 1908 at 8 A.M. Lt. Humphreys made first solo in a military plane. Fifteen minutes later Lt. Lahm soloed to become the second officer to learn to fly in a military plane, and both were at College Park, Marylnad.

B
Maj. General Benjamin D. Foulois (ret.) and Maj. Gen. Victor A. Conrad at historic marker unveiled at Ft. Sam Houston Texas. USAF Photo

C
Lt. Foulois and O. G. Simmons (rear) in Texas. Smithsonian Photo

A-Rex Smith landing his airplane on the mall near the Washington Monument on a flight from College Park. Smithsonian Photo

B-The Bleriot monoplane in front of the Rex Smith hangar. NAEMC Photo

"COLUMBIA" MONOPLANE. Rear View

C-The Columbia monoplane, rear view, at College Park. NAEMC Photo

"COLUMBIA" MONOPLANE

D-The Columbia monoplane, front view, with Simmons propeller. Mr. Paul Peck at controls. NAEMC Photo

E-Lincoln Beachey's Curtiss with 80 Grome engine. Note the seat belt safety device. WSAF Photo

F-The Grome engine in Bechey's craft is one of the first to appear at College Park in May 1913. USAF Photo

A
The Curtiss Model "D" two place pusher, Signal Corps Airplane No. 2 purchased by the Army in June 1911 was flown at College Park. USAF Photo

B
Wright Model "L" 60 h.p., 6 cylinder engine, 1916. USAF Photo

C
Burgess Dunne Training Plane, 1916. Note V-shaped wings and fuselage. USAF Photo

Curtiss Tractor Type used by
U.S. Army School and designed
by Loening, 1913. USAF Photo

B
Another Curtiss Tractor, Military type, winter 1912-13. Note
covered engine cowl, three-
bladed prop, and aviators
headgear. USAF Photo

C
Burgess aircraft and the begin-
ning of the covered fuselage.
Natl. Archives.

A
Curtiss Model "N" Military
Tractor. Training skid under
nose to prevent noseover on
student landings. USAF Photo

B
"Turk" Gardner in leather
flight gear. These old jennys
were equipped with 150 H.P.
Hisso Engine. NAEMC Photo

C-Revved up and ready for takeoff. NAEMC Photo

D-Planes were not equipped with wheel brakes so it was
necessary to have someone hold the wing in order to turn
about for taxiing. NAEMC Photo

A-1911 Curtiss Pusher and 1928 Curtiss A-3 in a unique side by side photo. USAF Photo

B-Old Jenny fuselage with a Grome engine and aerodynamic gas tanks on upper wing. NAEMC Photo

C-Research continued on another modified Jenny, this time with two Grome engines. Upper wing was braced up to support the extra weight. NAEMC Photo

D-This tri-motored transport was reported to have landed at College Park during an emergency. NAEMC Photo

E-The Christmas Bullet, named after its inventor & designer, Dr. William Whitney Christmas, was tested, sold, and flown at College Park. NAEMC Photo

F-Even the Marines have landed at College Park #7020 U.S. Marines in what looks like a 2 passenger Boeing F2B Comet. NAEMC Photo

A-Steve Reese and his Curtiss Robin with a Challenger Engine operated the passenger service at College Park for many years. NAEMC Photo

B-A lineup of planes, hangars and cars at CP in the late '30s. MNCPPC Photo

C-Over the fender view of aircraft of all types at College Park. NAEMC Photo

D-Even the old DC-3 frequented the field. NAEMC Photo

A
The Burrelli Loadmaster lands at College Park, July 20, 1957 to show its short takeoff & landing capabilities. The emblem on the side of the fuselage is not an airforce star but a delta or arrow point with a pair of golden wings on either side of the red ball. The planes entire fuselage between engines is a lifting wing configuration. NAEMC Photo

B
Even the Goodyear Blimp made College Park its headquarters while operating in the area each year. NAEMC Photo

C
Helicopters were nothing new at College Park since Berliner's experiments in the early 20's, but it was here that George Brinkerhoff taught Arthur Godfrey to fly a Hughs helicopter. Godfrey has never forgotten his College Park friends and used his morning radio programs to sound the call to "Save the Airport." NAEMC Photo

Chapter V
The Berliner Story

Just after the turn of the century, when inventing was very popular, father and son inventors Emile and Henry Berliner began a new endeavor. Emile Berliner had already made two fortunes with his patents on a plastic phonogaph record and player and with acoustical tile. This new idea was inspired by Henry who, at the age of fourteen, had ridden a short distance on a man-carrying kite and was also inspired by the fact that his mother had flown as a passenger of Mt. Titcum at College Park many years before. Nevertheless, both the Berliner's were intrigued with the idea of making a helicopter.

Their work commenced in the Gyro Motor Co. located near Sherman and Gerard Aves. in D.C., an automobile firm which they owned. An air-cooled Grome engine was used as the power source, and the counter rotating propellors had been custom-made by another inventor and craftsman, Mr. Spencer Heath.

Mr. Heath's claim to fame was the American Propeller and Mfg. Co. of Baltimore which produced the famous "Paragon Propel-lers." His factory was the first to mechanically mass produce propellers in America. His later achievements included making the propellers for the NC-3 and 4 and inventing a variable pitch propeller that was automatically controlled by the speed of the engine.

The first test flights of the A & B versions were at Corby's Place in Rockville, Maryland on part of the golf course. Because more testing room was needed and also a larger hangar was needed, they moved to College Park in early 1920. The following photographs, taken from his photographic album, show the many versions and changes in their invention until their final success in 1924, nine years before the Sikorsky helicopter was invented. The Berliner Helicopter was the FIRST helicopter to fly with maneuvering capabilities. Many other inventors had built helicopters which went straight up or down or that were tethered to the ground but until this time none was capable of controlled flight.

A-Inventors Emile (left) and son Henry (right) with one of their early version helicopters. NAEMC Photo

B-A close-up view of the Grome engine and controls which started their experiments. NAEMC Photo

C-Model A in test flights which they found very unstable at Corby's Place in Rockville, Md. NAEMC Photo

D-Model B. Another rudder and outrigger skids were added to prevent it from turning over. NAEMC Photo

A-Model C venetian blind type louvers were added to further increase the stability. Henry Berliner at controls. NAEMC Photo

B-Model D. A rudder was added aft for directional control. The experiments were moved to College Park for more flying space. NAEMC Photo

C-Flag flies over government air mail service building at College Park as Henry is photographed with his Model D. NAEMC Photo

D-A rear view of the D Model. NAEMC Photo

E-Front view of the D Model. NAEMC Photo

F-Henry with his two mechanics W. Tom Queen and Herbert Fahy. NAEMC Photo

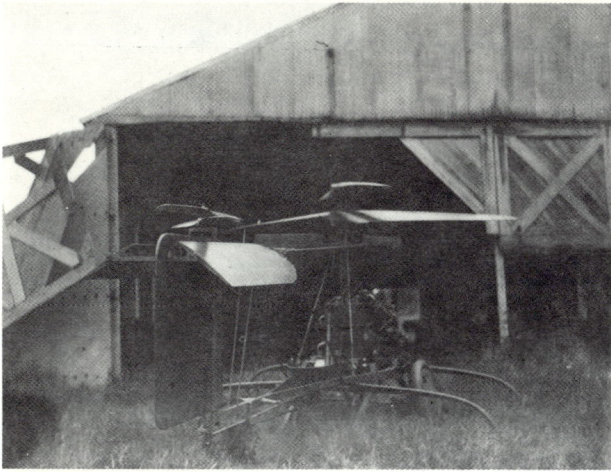

A-A smaller set of counter rotating blades is added above the rudder in the E version.

B-Blades are dropped below the rudder in this F version called the "Grass cutter" for obvious reasons. NAEMC Photo

C-The Rex Smith Hangar looks abandoned as the mechanics make a few minor adjustments. NAEMC Photo

D-After limited success a fuselage is added to the "G" version with twin sets of blades including a small stabilizer prop just in front of the tail section. NAEMC Photo

E-With father Emile looking on, Henry and crew roll the "H" version onto the field for its tests. Three wings have been added. NAEMC Photo

F-As the engine starts up we get a closer look at the "H" version with Henry at the controls. NAEMC Photo

A-This aerial view of the "G" version shows its overall design.
NAEMC Photo

B-Mechanics are so confident they follow behind with hands in pockets. NAEMC Photo

C-This test shot shows the water tower and army barracks and stable constructed on the field for the enlisted men. Henry flies about 12 feet high for 100 yards turns and returns to starting place to prove its maneuverability. NAEMC Photo

A-A short while after his helicopter experiments (which he successfully demonstrated for the pentagon officials), Henry turned his talents toward building a seaplane. This plane worked as well in the air as on the water. The craft was powered by an inverted outboard motor with modifications in the drive shaft and the water cooler. The "flying boat" as he called it, was tested on the Potomac near Blue Plains about 1924 or 25. The engine was very hard to start but the plane flew like a dream. Maybe it was because of his experience in building 25 to 30 OX-5 planes before starting this project.

However, as the story goes, one day Mr. Curtiss was trying to demonstrate his seaplane for the Navy on the Potomac. Mr. Berliner saw that he was having trouble getting his plane started so he taxied out to see if he could be of assistance. When he approached Mr. Curtiss and observed all the military officers standing along the shore he became even more concerned. Mr. Curtiss annoyed by his appearance at this time in a seaplane, tried to motion him to stay away — go back — get lost — and finally shook his fist at Henry. At this point Henry, not to be slighted, took off and buzzed, circled, and dove at the Curtiss plane. However, the roar of his engine kept him from hearing the swear words Mr. Curtiss was shouting at him. This is how Berliner was said to have flown circles around Curtiss. NAEMC Photo

A
Henry didn't stop with his seaplane but went on to develop the world's first all-metal smooth skin aircraft. This plane was the prototype of the Aircoupe, the plane that wouldn't tailspin. NAEMC Photo

B
This plane was test flown at College Park by putting it in a 9G drive, and the wing stayed on when it pulled out. The X on the tail was a marker for experimental craft. NAEMC Photo

C
Standing in front of the sunken gas tanks at College Park you can easily see her clean smooth lines. NAEMC Photo

Chapter VI
Oscar L. Mote

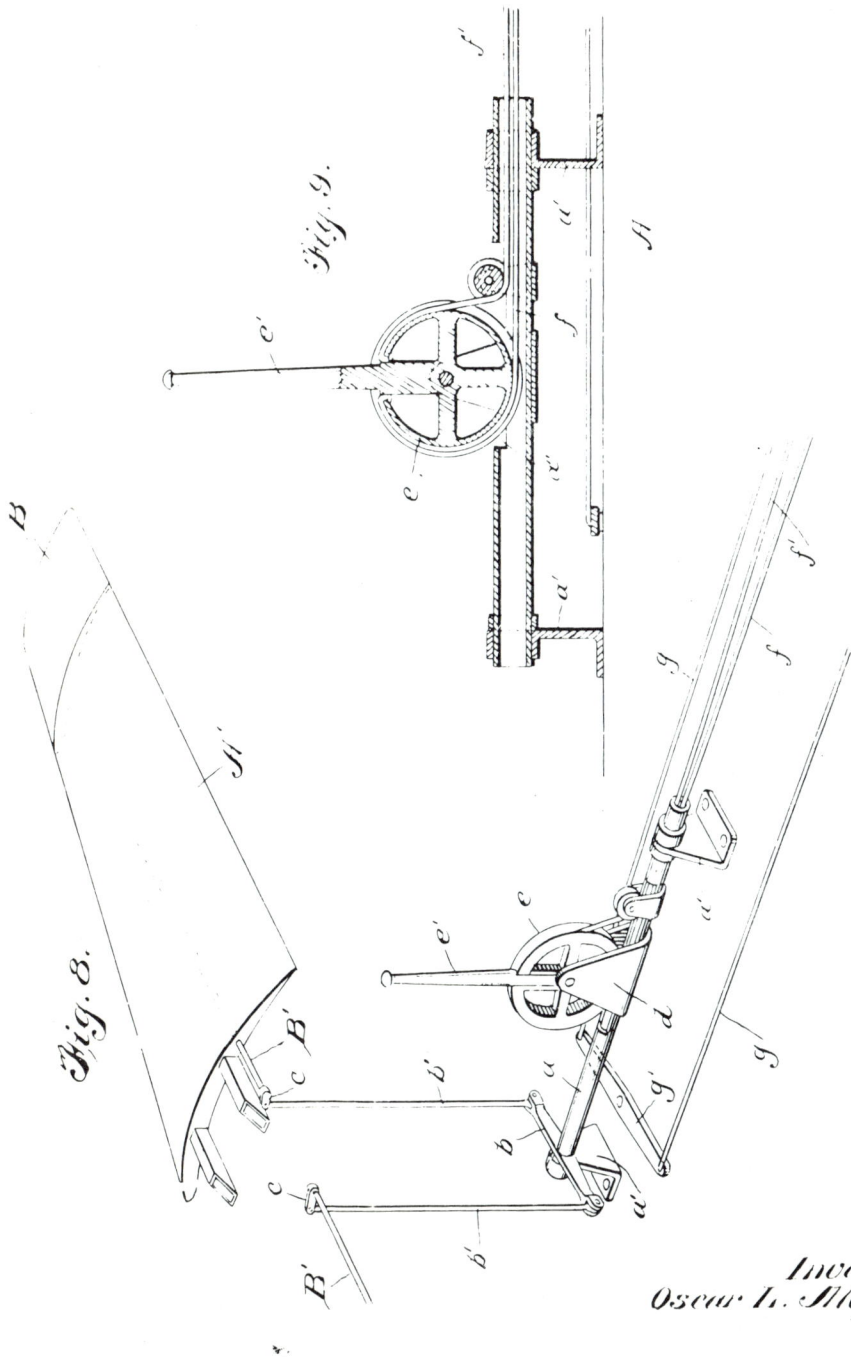

Fig. 9.

Fig. 8.

Inventor
Oscar L. Mote

Atty

Oscar L. Mote is another of those forgotten inventors. Mr. Mote spent many years as an aviation mechanic at College Park with the Wrights, Rex Smith, "Hap" Arnold and Henry Berliner, the Pensacola Naval Air Station, the Curtiss Airplane Co. Buffalo, N.Y. and with the Aerostandard Co. of New Jersey. Though he was highly praised by all the pilots for whom he worked, his real accomplishment was his invention of the "Joy Stick" used to control early aircraft. Shown here is the patent drawing and on the following page you will see the models he built of it. It was a single control that did the work of four previous devices. January 29, 1919 was the date shown on the patent model.

Mr. Mote also designed his own plane shown in photographs 51B and C. The model that appears in 51A was built for Mr. Thomas L. Eggleston of Erid, Oklahoma, which was to be the world's first commercial global transport. This design employed aerodynamic lifting wing struts which gave it greater stability and lift.

On page 52 you will find a poem by Mr. Mote which was presented to Maj. Gen. H. "Hap" Arnold, Chief of the Air Corps on May 20, 1940, which he said "brought back fond memories of early flyers and many of my old friends."

A-Mr. Mote in an old Jenny. NAEMC Photo

B-The patent model built by a master craftsman. NAEMC Photo

C-All control surfaces on this model actually work from the
miniature "Joy Stick" inside. NAEMC Photo

D-A close-up view of the patent device. NAEMC Photo

A
The Eggleston Air Ship Model built by Mr. Mote back when Calvert Road, seen in the background, wasn't even paved, July 2, 1927. NAEMC Photo

B
The Mote Plane without engine at Mineola, N.Y. NAEMC Photo

C
March 23, 1911 Aircraft Show at Mineola, N.Y. where Mr. Mote sold his first plane to Mr. Herrick Aiken of Lawrence, Mass. NAEMC Photo

AIR CASTLES

by

O. L. Mote

The past few years seem but moments,
As the days fly swiftly by,
When the world gave to its children
That great desire, to fly.

We had dreamed of this for ages,
Men had studied and worked in vain,
But our inventions were not successful
Until the good old Wright type came.

And to them we owe our gratitude,
For 'twas they who gave it birth,
The greatest of all achievements,
To soar above the earth.

There was Langley, Chinutte and Lilenthal,
And hosts of others, too,
Who tried to solve the problem,
But their airplanes never flew.

Then the Wright brothers went to Kitty-hawk,
A well named and chosen place,
And carried on their experiments,
Until they flew off into space.

Then a few short moments afterwards
Came Curtiss, Bleriot, and Farman,
Rex Smith and Captain Baldwin,
Harry Harkness and Clifford B. Harmon.

Louis Paulhan and Hubert Latham,
"Tony" Jannus and dear old Peck,
"Tod" Schriver and Charles K. Hamilton,
Milling, Arnold and Captain Beck.

Beachey, Hoxey, and Johnstone,
"Bud" Mars, John Frisbie and Hilliard,
Harriet Quimby and Cecil Peoli,
Brindley, Beatty, and Charles P. Williard.

"Bill" Badger and St. Croix Johnson,
Ruth Law and her brother "Rod",
Katherine and Marjorie Stinson,
And many others which I've forgot.

Since then great changes have been wrought,
And the old familiar faces
Of nearly all the veteran flyers
Are stamped on memories' pages.

They gave their lives to science,
That all the world might profit,
For they were heroes, one and all,
And the world has ne'er forgot it.

We've all seen many changes,
In construction and design,
From the pusher type of nineteen eight
To the planes which crossed the Rhine

Now Langley tried a tandem type
With the wings set fore and aft,
While Wrights tried a twin screw biplane,
Which proved a sturdy craft.

Curtiss flew a pusher type,
With single surfaced wings
Which won the world's first trophy
At the international meet at Rheims.

Then Bleriot built a Monoplane,
With a single tractor screw,
Which made his reputation,
When o'er the Channel it flew.

Then still another type appeared,
It's the Curtiss flying boat,
And for pleasure and enjoyment
There's no better craft afloat.

Then came the war in foreign lands,
With which none other can compare,
And the fighting of our pilots brave,
Have won the conquest of the air.

And with the Armistice at hand,
And victory nearly won,
We've taught the world what we could do,
In the conquering of the "Hun".

And when the world's at peace again,
And things have quieted down,
We'll find the sturdy battle-plane,
Just flying from town to town.

Delivering all our Christmas gifts,
And New Year's presents, too,
By aerial mail and air express,
Gee, won't Santa-Claus feel blue?

And when it comes to honey-moons,
We'll hunt Dan Cupid in his lair,
For we'll make these trips by Aeroplanes
Which are truly "Aircastles of the Air".

Chapter VII
The Air Mail Service

College Park Airport was the Washington terminus of the worlds first regularly scheduled air mail service. Military pilots first demonstrated that the mail could be moved quicker by air than by trains. President Woodrow Wilson was on hand to greet Maj. Reuben H. Fleet at the Potomac Field Hangar, May 15, 1918 upon his arrival. Having proved their point the Postmaster General, Mr. A. L. Burleson, was instructed to establish our nation's first regularly scheduled commercial air mail service. This service began at College Park on August 12th, 1918 and went north to Philadelphia and New York.

The Post Office Department, having secured another $100,000, contracted with the Standard Aircraft Co. for six made-to-order planes to carry the mail. On August 6, 1918 the delivery was made; this marked another aviation milestone; these were the first aircraft ever built specifically for transporting payload purposes.

April 12 thru April 26, 1918 Oscar L. Mote worked on planes at the Polo Grounds and in the hangar when the army was carrying the mail from Potomac Field. On December 18, 1918, Mr. Mote applied and was hired to work for the Air Mail Service at College Park. Mr. Mote had just left the Standard Aircraft Co. after two and one-half years as General Superintendent of their Experimental Department, which made the above-mentioned planes for the Post Office Department.

Below is pictured Gen. Benjamin D. Foulois, of earlier College Park History, standing in front of Air Maps showing the expanded routes covered by February 1934. USAF Photo

A

Old Air Mail Plane #1 was commissioned to carry the mail from College Park.

A local artist was employed to paint an emblem on the side of the fuselage but was unable to originate an acceptable idea. The pilot, looking down at the ground observed an old mail pouch tobacco bag, handed it to the artist and said paint something like this. Upon returning to the plane a short while later, sure enough, it read Mail Pouch Tobacco. No! No! No! exclaimed the pilot, it has to read U.S. Mail, and that's how she received her emblem. Also note the number 1 behind the cockpit. U.S .Post Office Photo

B
Air Mail Plane #1 take off from College Park amid the noise of the engine, a trail of dust, and the cheers of hundreds of spectators. Smithsonian Photo

C
Loading the mail at College Park in 1919 is a DeHavlin DH-4 parked near the compass-rose which is still visible today at the airport. U.S. Post Office Photo

A
Old 256 rests quietly at College Park between flights. They were rigid and slow but dependable. U.S. Post Office Photo

B
At the 25th Anniversary of the Air Mail Service at College Park, many old planes and aviators reassembled for a gala reunion on August 12, 1943. Smithsonian Photo

C
At the 50th Anniversary of the Air Mail Service only one old plane remains. Pictured here from left to right are Dr. Paul Garber, J. Kenneth Lewis, Dana E. DeHart and Fred C. Knaver on August 12, 1968 standing beside old 249 in the last hangar at College Park. Smithsonian Photo

HER FINAL FLIGHT INTO HISTORY

PARADE AND

AIR SHOW

AUG. 10, 11, 12   10 AM – 5 PM

U.S. AIR MAIL SERVICE
50 YEARS
1918-1968
COLLEGE PARK AIRPORT

COLLEGE PARK AIRPORT OUR NATIONS FIRST MARYLAND

Aircraft Display & Exhibits MILITARY, CIVILIAN, N.A.S.A. (New & Old)

Airplane & Helicopter Rides BAND MUSIC, DRILL TEAMS, MOVIES

Sky Diving GLIDER DEMONSTRATIONS, MODEL AIRPLANE & ROCKET FLYING

LOCATED BETWEEN U.S.-1 and KENILWORTH AVE. ON CALVERT ROAD, COLLEGE PARK, MD.

FOR FURTHER INFORMATION WRITE OR CALL: College Park AIR SHOW, Box 1909 zip 20740

Phone 301-779-1909 or 277-4055

If you plan to fly in get your reservations TODAY! Airport will be closed to all air traffic

except EXHIBITORS and RESERVATION HOLDERS.

Reproduction of the 50th Anniversary Air Show poster.

NAEMC Photo

Chapter VIII
The Battle For Survival

A
As if it weren't bad enough that age and time were spoiling her beauty, the lack of concern by her owners and tenants was also degrading. Her runways were muddy and bumpy. The hangars were rusty and falling apart. To complicate matters a Hurricane named Hazel added the crowning blow. College Park Airport was dying. Construction crews dumped fill debris in her tie down areas, and local citizens started dumping their garbage and old automobiles there. Didn't anyone care about her? About the many valiant men and deeds she held record to? It was all so hopeless. Photographs courtesy Claude Moorse

A-The operations building was losing her roof, windows were broken, walls were bulging and ivy was crawling up her walls, and she was surrounded by weeds. NAEMC Photo

B-There were no fences to keep dragsters off her runways. NAEMC Photo

C-Her parking lot was mud holes. NAEMC Photo

D-There was an open well behind the ops building that any child could have fallen into. NAEMC Photo

E-The old W.A.F.S. & C.A.P. Building was so bad you would fall through the floor if you dared enter. NAEMC Photo

F-Even some planes on the field were unkept. NAEMC Photo

A-Planes left abandoned were vandalized. C. Morse Photo

B-It appeared more like a junk yard than an airport. C. Morse Photo

C-Inside the ops building the roof leaked and the ceiling was falling. NAEMC Photo

D-Combustible materials were all over the place. NAEMC Photo

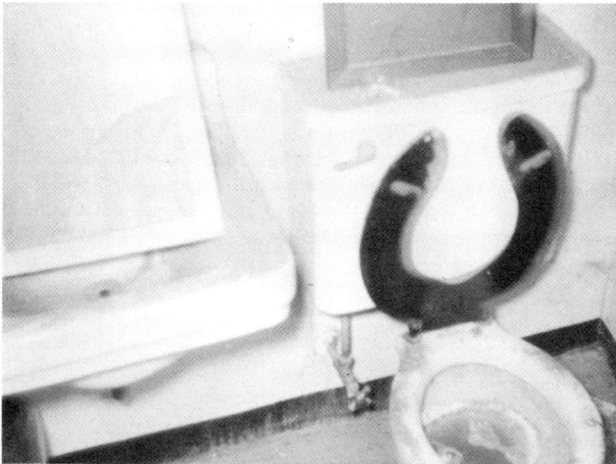

E-The rest room was unfit for human use. NAEMC Photo

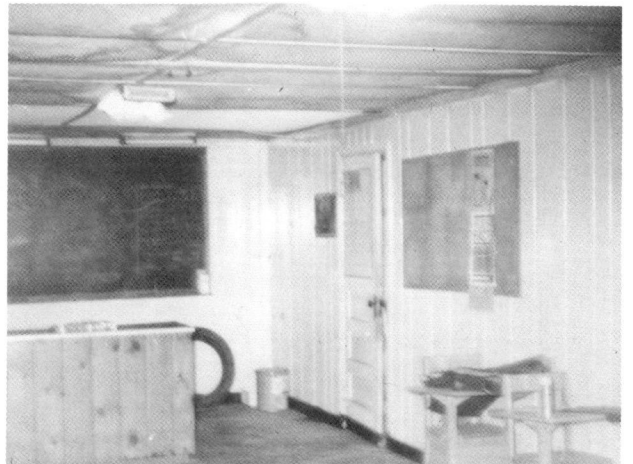

F-The Flight Lounge was a disgrace. NAEMC Photo

A-July 30, 1957. The Early Birds flocked to a meeting at the airport. Among those present were: Gen. Frank P. Lahm, Walter L. Brock, Robert J. Armor, Gen. T. D. Milling, Paul Culver, Dr. Paul Garber, D. H. Young. Nearly 55 in all came to reminisce the good old days when they flew here. The Early Birds heard from Chairman Fred C. Knaver of the Committee for Perpetuation of the College Park Airport. His famous quote was: "If we're going to make history, let's preserve it." Many yarns about the "crates" that they flew filled the air. Retiring president David H. Young of The Early Birds read a proposed citation which was part of a plaque that was erected at the field later that year.

If there was ever a knight on a white horse, Fred Knaver deserves that title. His undaunting and relentless efforts to save the College Park Airport are almost legendary. No task was too insurmountable, no contact too insignificant. From meetings on Capitol Hill to cutting weeds on the field, Fred is always on the job. It was through Fred's efforts that Congressman Richard E. Langford's bill to put the Smithsonian Air & Space Museum at College Park almost succeeded, but for a veto by President Eisenhower at the last monument. Even this book is due in part to his dedicated efforts.

A-Loving Helicopter Service was the first to take steps to repair the airport. They completely refurbished the last remaining hangar into a bright, shiny building. NAEMC Photo

B-My suggestion for preserving the airfield was to build a National Aerospace Educational Memorial Center, being viewed here by: L. to R.: Mr. Dutton, Former Mayor Gullett, Col. Reese (ret), Bill Yoho, and B. J. Desnoyers. NAEMC Photo

C-Members of the National Aerospace Cadets played an important roll in cleaning and fixing up the old field. NAEMC Photo

D-There two cadets Lou Wallack and Wayne Russ remove the small poorly lettered sign marking the airport's entrance. NAEMC Photo

E-This new sign was erected in place of the old one. NAEMC Photo

F-Thousands of these leaflets designed by artist Milton Coniff who draws Steve Canyon were distributed by NAEMC members and are still available. NAEMC Photo

A-Here comes the parade, leading off the 50th Anniversary of Air Mail Service. College Park celebrated with a three-day gala air show. NAEMC Photo

B-Flag raising and the Star Spangled Banner at the Calvert Road Monument next to the Maryland National Capital Park and Planning Commission offices. NAEMC Photo

C-Immediately following the flag ceremony there was a fly over by jets of the local Air National Guard Unit from Andrews A.F.B. NAEMC Photo

D-Dr. Paul Garber of the Smithsonian Air & Space Museum headed up an outstanding group of speakers who all supported the preservation of an operating airport at College Park. NAEMC Photo

E-Miss College Park Airport (Joy Holland) was selected as Queen of the three-day spectacular. Here she greets Ken Kuhn of College Park as he sits in his homemade biplane. NAEMC Photo

F-College Park Air Show was a huge success as thousands flock to witness the aerial pagentry. NAEMC Photo

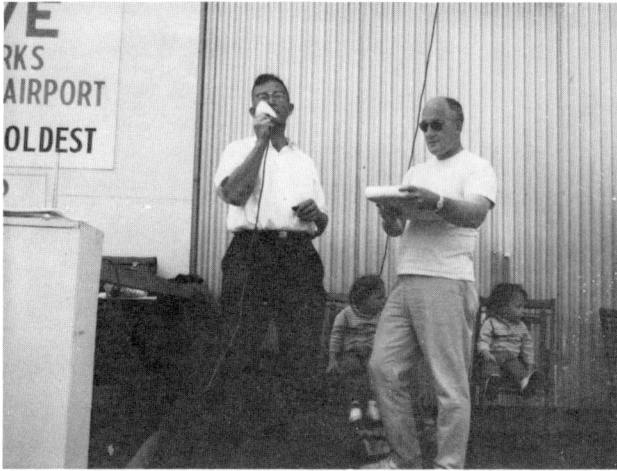

A-Ken Lewis, President of the NAEMC, announces another happening as then mayor William Gullett prepares to read the city's proclamation. NAEMC Photo

B-Ken Kuhn receives the mail from local postmaster's representative as he prepares to fly special commemorative air mail card from College Park to Baltimore on this 50th Anniversary of Air Mail Service. NAEMC Photo

C-Mrs. Harold J. Crelly, former postmaster of College Park, and her husband remember the Wright Brothers and the early army officers at College Park with whom they played cards while waiting for the train. NAEMC Photo

D-Members of the Maryland Sky Diving Team who performed their precision skill that thrilled the crowds at the air show. NAEMC Photo

E-1966 Air photo shows the nearness of the College Park Airport to the University of Maryland. NAEMC Photo

F-Another '66 air view showing the industrial encroachment on the field. The east-west runway has already been closed. NAEMC Photo

A-Henry Berliner greets Mrs. Ken Lewis at College Park's big air show while her husband (center) looks on. Mr. Berliner, inventor of the helicopter built at College Park, was one of the special guests of the day. NAEMC Photo

B-Ken Kuhn's home built experimental biplane. NAEMC Photo

C-The Navy's NARTU Trainer is not the first navy plane to visit the field. NAEMC Photo

D-Two Army Sikorsky Helicopters were a popular attraction at the show. NAEMC Photo

E-Executive Aviation did a land office business at the show, giving many persons their first flight in a helicopter. NAEMC Photo

Chapter IX
College Park Today

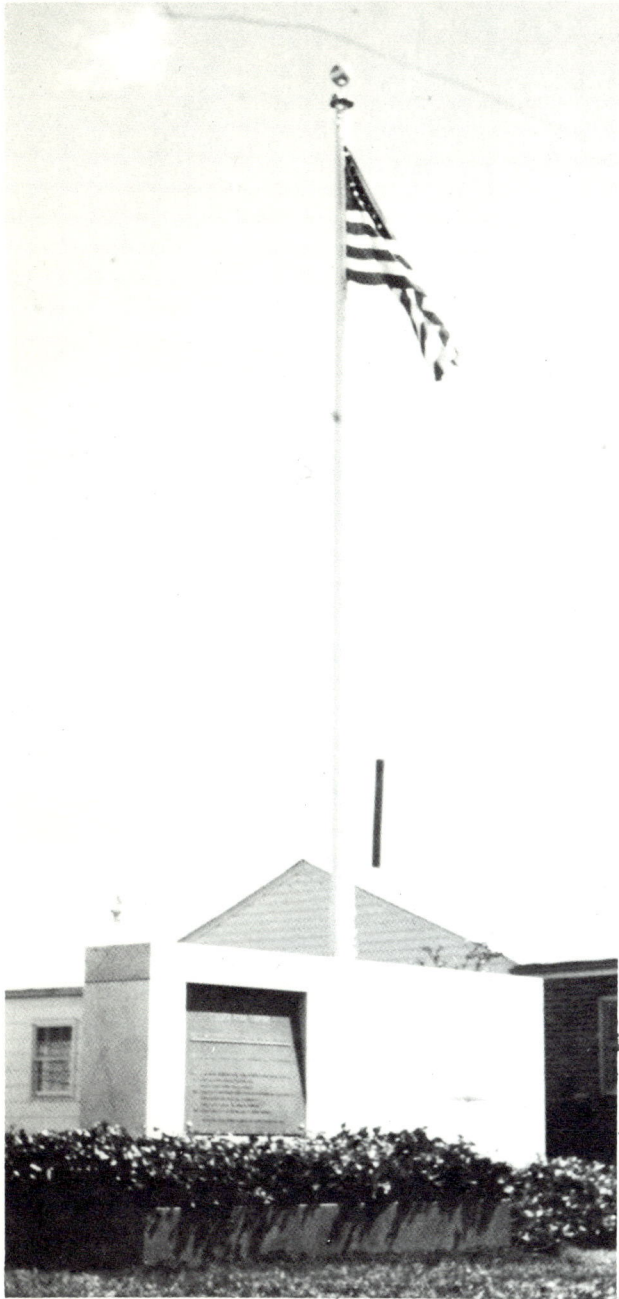

In 1961 the College Park Rotary Club, Eugene Chaney, President, erected this beautiful marker and flag pole to the many notable events which occurred on this airfield. It is located on Calvert Road near the Maryland-National Capital Park and Planning Commission's Maintenance and Development Office.

On August 22, 1967 in a proclamation by the Mayor and City Council of the City of College Park are desires of continuing the operations of this historic airport and the erection of a museum and historical center without creating a tax burden to the residents of College Park; they ordered that the National Aerospace Educational Memorial Center, Inc., be recognized and proclaimed the official fund raising organization to acquire the airport and to continue its operations and develop a museum and educational center in cooperation with residents and the city government of College Park.

The State of Maryland on March 6, 1968, passed House Resolution No. 89 honoring the City of College Park for its efforts to preserve the College Park Airport and called on all interested persons in the state and nation to cooperate in the efforts to save the Airport and also listed many of the accomplishments which occurred there.

February 20, 1973 Prince Georges County Executive William Gullett and the County Commissioners purchased the land for 1.5 million dollars and conveyed the land to the Maryland-National Capital Park and Planning Commission to provide for its continued use as an operating airport, museum and educational center.

Today, thanks to the Maryland-National Capital Area Park and Planning Commission the airport has a new look. The tie down areas are kept trim and neat like a golf course, the buildings have been repaired, fences have been erected and even picnic tables have been added so visitors can enjoy themselves while visiting this historic field. There is even a beginning of a small museum there, where many of the old historic memorabilia is on exhibit. NAEMC Photo

A-The hangar has a new large sign. Ken Lewis Photo

B-The property is now part of our park service. Ken Lewis Photo

C-The Ops Building is neat & attractive. Ken Lewis Photo

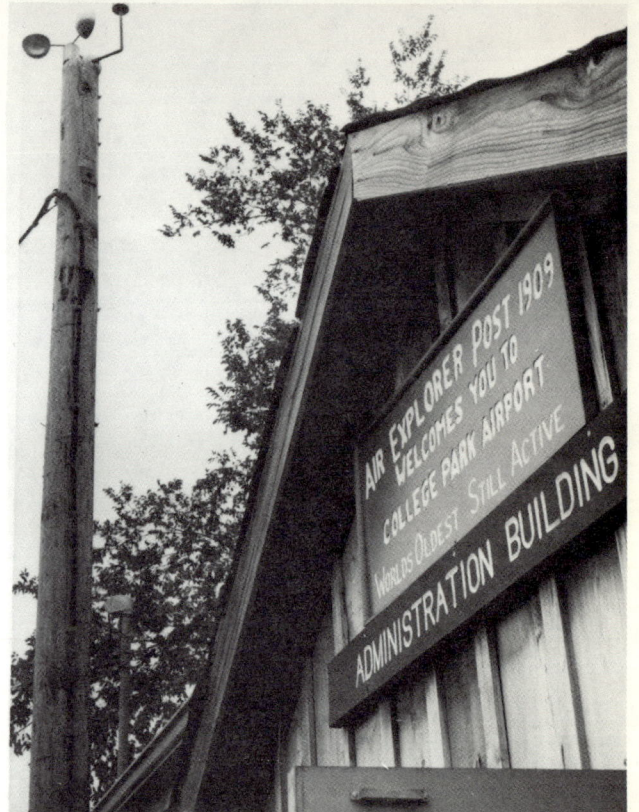

D-Air Explorer Post 1909 is using it for education purposes. Ken Lewis Photo

E-The airport is restful for tourists. Ken Lewis Photo

F-The Airport is being operated like a professional business. Ken Lewis Photo

A-The office has Unicom ground to air 122.80 MHZ radio contact with arriving and departing planes. Ken Lewis Photo

B-A flight information center is up-to-date with the latest weather and flight maps and even a "tale-spin lounge" for relaxing or waiting. Ken Lewis Photo

C-All planes are tied down and under constant surveillance. Ken Lewis Photo

D-The historic old "Compass-Rose" has been carefully preserved. Ken Lewis Photo

E-New directional markers are on the taxi strip. Ken Lewis Photo

F-Service facilities are available and mechanics are on duty to assist where needed. Ken Lewis Photo

Today this small and friendly air field has a paved and lighted runway, and it is as safe as any in the nation. It is limited in size but is large enough to handle small private aircraft. If the Wright Brothers could see it now I'm sure they too would be proud of it. We should take our hats off to all the men, women and children who donated their time and energy to preserve this hallowed ground for future generations. Our special thanks should also go to those elected officials who stood their ground and fought to preserve one of our American heritages.

Chapter X
Future Plans For College Park Airport

A

The original plan for the National Aerospace Educational Memorial was to be a center containing not only the memorabilia of College Park Airport but a permanent home for a large collection of over 1,000 plastic model airplanes through which the history of man's achievement in air could be visually seen in a short period of time. It was also to have contained a large aerospace library and even a large number of aviation paintings and reprints. NAEMC Photo

National Aerospace Education Memorial Center

B

The second proposed was even more in keeping with the historic society ideas of restoring the original 6 hangars to look exactly as they did about 1912, but which on the inside would be a museum and art gallery. The planes on the field would be permanently anchored to give visitors a close look at many of the historic planes tucked away now at Silver Hill, Md. as part of the Smithsonian collection. NAEMC Photo

C

In cooperation with the University and Prince Georges County Board of Education, an Aerospace Vocational School could be established to teach students, both high school and college, many of the trades in the aerospace industry. The control tower would be used only to train future control tower operators and not as part of the airport. NAEMC Photo

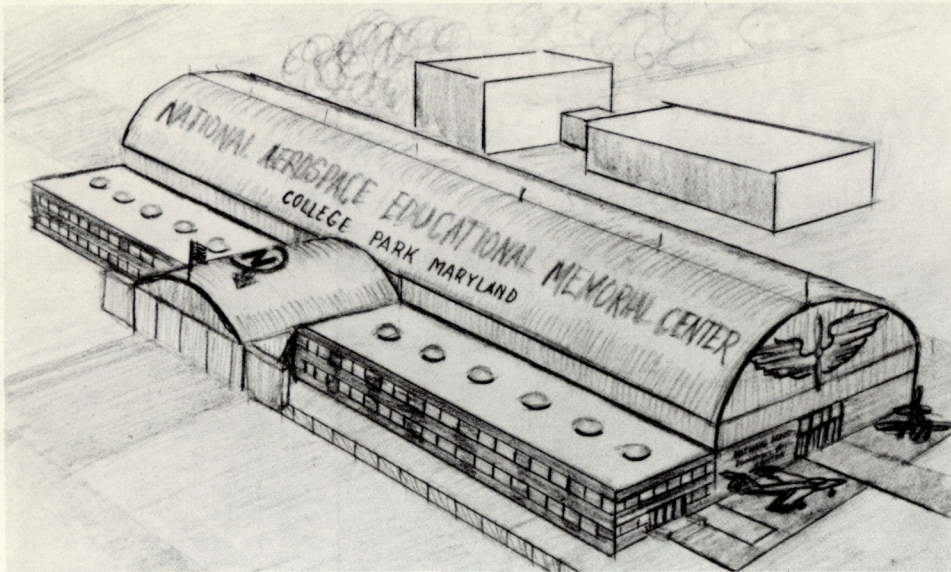

A
Looking ahead into the future, if money were available, a large hangar could be built to house historic planes that cannot be left outside in the weather. The smaller hangar on the side is where vocational students under proper guidance could help restore old planes for the museum, either outdoor or indoor types. The long flat buildings would be classrooms and shops and barracks for summer cadet programs. Artist Concept

B
If at some future date all these ideas could be incorporated, the airport would look something like this sketch which I have done. The fenced-in area would very much limit the number of planes that could be tied down here, but it would become more of a tourist attraction to visitors. The airport, however, must always be kept as an operating airport to retain its title. Artist Concept

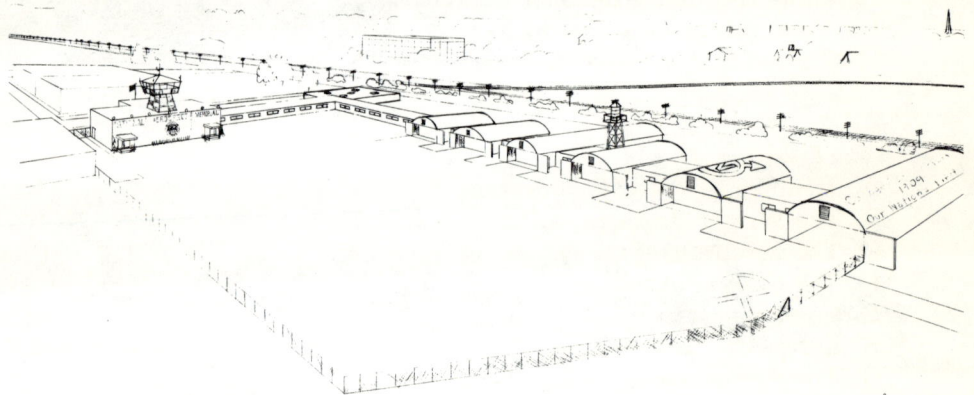

C
If, and it is a big if, all the aircraft at the Smithsonian's Silver Hill repository were loaned to College Park this is how the Museum would possibly look. Regardless of what anyone has plans or dreams of, only the cooperative efforts of dedicated people can make it happen. Can we count on your support? Artist Concept

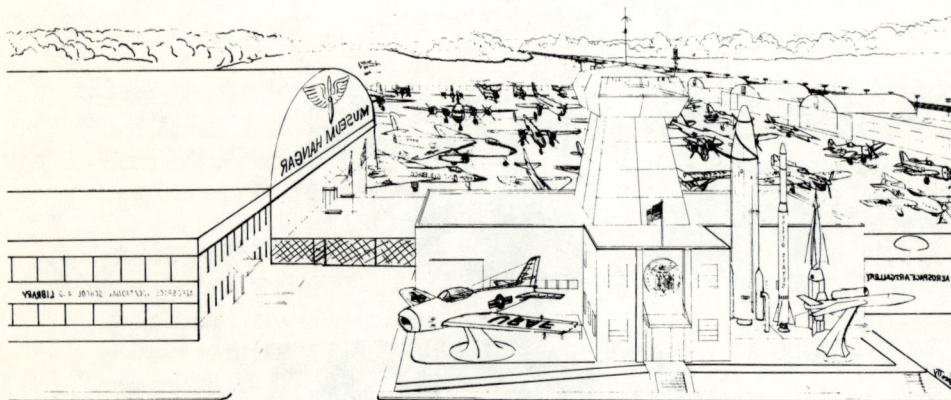

Bibliography

The information in this book has been collected from a wide variety of sources. Each source is preceded by a number, and each photograph has already been credited and given a page number and alphabetical letter from top to bottom (example, 17B: page 17, 2nd picture), as you would read a book. To locate the source, simply use the list of photograph numbers and the numbers which follow indicating all the sources of reference on that subject.

Sources

1. United States Air Force Still Photograph Repository, Alexandria, Va.
2. Dr. Paul Garber, Smithsonian Air & Space Museum, Wash., D.C.
3. United States Archives, Washington, D.C.
4. Maryland-National Capital Park & Planning Commission, Prince Georges County, Md.
5. National Aerospace Educational Memorial Center, College Park, Md.
6. Reference books from the personal collection of the author (see book title code)*
7. Individual person gave photo for use in book (name given)
8. From the Oscar L. Mote Collection.
9. From the Henry Berliner Collection
10. From a tape recording by person or persons involved, firsthand account.
11. United States Post Office Dept. Exhibit and Displays Branch

* List of the author's resource books from his library of over 2,800 books & magazines.

Title	Author
A. How We Invented the Airplane	Orville Wright
B. The Wright Brothers — Pioneers of American Aviation	Quentin Reynolds
C. The Invention of the Aeroplane 1799-1909	Charles H. Gibbs-Smith
D. The Story of Aviation	David C. Cooke
E. Contact — The Story of the Early Birds	Henry Serrano Villard
F. Early Air Pioneers 1862-1935	Maj. James F. Sunderman, USAF
G. The Aeroplane — An Historical Survey	Charles H. Gibbs-Smith
H. A Brief History of Flying — From Myth to Space Travel	Charles H. Gibbs-Smith
I. A Chronology of World Aviation	Lt. Col. Gene Gurney, USAF
J. Man Unafraid — The Miracle of Military Aviation	Stephen F. Tillman
K. How Our Army Grew Wings	Chandler & Lahm
L. Army Flyer	H. H. Arnold & Ira C. Eaker
M. A History of the United States Air Force 1907-1957	Alfred Goldberg
N. The Compact History of the United States Air Force	Carroll V. Glines, Jr.
O. From the Wright Brothers to the Astronauts — The Memoris of Maj. Gen. Benjamin D. Foulois	Benjamin D. Foulois
P. Ceiling Unlimited	Lloyd Morris & Kendall Smith
Q. Color Profiles of World War I Combat Planes	Dale McAdoo
R. Federal Aviation Agency Historical Fact Book 1926-63	Arnold E. Briddon & Ellmore A. Champie
S. Fledgelings — Pioneers In Aviation	Columbia Historical Soc.
T. The World's First Aeroplane Flights	C. H. Gibbs-Smith
U. Pioneers of Flight	Henry T. Wallhouser
V. This Was Air Travel	Henry R. Palmer, Jr.
W. The American Heritage History of Flight	Editors of American Heritage & Arthur Gordon
X. The Challenging Skies	C. R. Roseberry
Y. New Horizon Book of Flying	Robert Blockburn
Z. The Complete Book of Helicopters	D. N. Ahnstrom
AA. Journal-American Aviation Historical Society (Fall '75)	Merle Olmsted

Bibliography Cross Reference Chart

Inside Cover-2
13A-1
13B-1
13C-1
13 copy-6-A, B, C, D, F, G, H, J
14A-1
14B-1
14C-1
15A-1, 6-J, M, O
15B-1, 6-J, M, O
15C-1, 6-J, M, O
15D-1, 6-J, M, O
15E-1, 6-J, M, O
15F-1, 6-J, M, O
16A-1, 6-A, B, C
16B-1, 6-A, B, C
16C-1, 6-A, B, C
17A-3
17B-1, 6-K, O
17C-1, 6-K, O
17D-1, 6-K, O
17 copy-6-F, N, 10, 6-A, B, C, K
18A-3, 6-K
18B-3-
18C-3, 6-A, B, C
19A-1, 6-K
19B-1, 6-O
19C-5, 7, 10
19D-5, 7, 10
20A-5, 7, 10
20B-5, 7, 10
20C-1
21A-5, 7, 10
21B-1, 6-AA
21C-1, 6-M
22A-1
22B-1
22C-1
22D-1
22E-1
22F-1
23A-1, 6-L
23B-1
23C-1
24A-1
24B-5
24C-1
25A-1
25B-1
25C-1, 6-J
26A-1
26B-1
26C-1
26D-1
26E-1
26F-1
27A-1, 2, 6-A, B, F, O, R, T
27B-1, 2, 6-A, B, F, J, K, L, O, R, T
27C-1, 2, 6-J, K, L, M, N
27D-1, 2, 3, 6-G, H, I, J, K, L, M, N

28A-1, 2, 6-D, F, G, I, J, K, L, M, N, O, P, T
28B-1, 2, 6-D, F, G, I, J, K, L, M, N, O, P, T
28C-1, 3, 6-O, 7, 10
29A-5
29B-11, 2
29C-5, 10
30A-1, 5, 7
30B-5
30C-1, 6-F, J, K, M, N, O
30D-1, 5, 7
30 copy-2, 3, 5, 6-J, M, N, 7, 8, 10
31A-5, 10
32A-5
32B-5, 10
32C-5, 10
32D-2
33A-1
33B-2, 5
33C-5, 7
33D-1
33E-5, 7
33F-5, 7
34A-2
34B-2
34C-2
35A-1, 6-J, K, L, M, N, O
35B-1, 6-O
35C-2, 6-O
36A-2, 10
36B-
36C-
36D-5, 7
36E-1
36F-1
37A-1
37B-1
37B-1
37C-1
38A-1
38B-1
38C-3
39A-1
39B-5, 7
39C-5, 7
39D-5, 7
40A-1
40B-5
40C-5
40D-5, 7
40E-5, 7, 10
40F-5, 7
41A-5, 7
41B-5, 7
41C-5, 7
41D-5, 7
42A-5, 7, 10
42B-5
42C-5, 7, 10
43 copy-5, 7, 10

43A-5, 7, 10
43B-5, 7, 10
43C-5, 7, 10
43D-5, 7, 10
44A-5, 7, 10
44B-5, 7, 10
44C-5, 7, 10
44D-5, 7, 10
44E-5, 7, 10
44F-5, 7, 10
45A-5, 7, 10
45B-5, 7, 10
45C-5, 7, 10
45D-5, 7, 10
45E-5, 7, 10
45F-5, 7, 10
46A-5, 7, 10
46B-5, 7, 10
46C-5, 7, 10
47 copy-5, 7, 10
48A-5, 7, 10
48B-5, 7, 10
48C-5, 7, 10
49 copy-5, 7, 10
49A-5, 7, 10
50A-5, 7, 10
50B-5, 7, 10
50C-5, 7, 10
50kd-5, 7, 10
51A-5, 7, 10
51B-5, 7, 10
51C-5, 7, 10
52 copy-5, 7
53A-5
53B-5
53C-1, 11
54A-11, 2
54B-2
54C-11
55A-11
55B-2, 11
55C-2, 11
56A-5
57-7
58A-5
58B-5
58C-5
58D-5
58E-5
58F-5, 1
59A-7
59B-7
59C-5
59D-5
59E-5
59F-5
60 copy-2, 7, 10
60A-2, 7, 10
60B-5, 7, 10
61A-5
61B-5
61C-5

61D-5
61E-5
61F-5
62A-5
62B-5
62C-5
62D-5
62E-5
62F-5
63A-5
63B-5
63C-5
63D-5
63E-5
63F-5
64A-5
64B-5
64C-5
64D-5
64E-5
65 copy-7
65A-5
65B-5
66A-5, 7
66B-5, 7
66C-5, 7
66D-5, 7
66E-5, 7
66F-5, 7
67A-5, 7
67B-5, 7
67C-5, 7
67D-5, 7
67E-5, 7
67F-5, 7
69A-5
69B-5
69C-5
70A-7
70B-7
70C-7